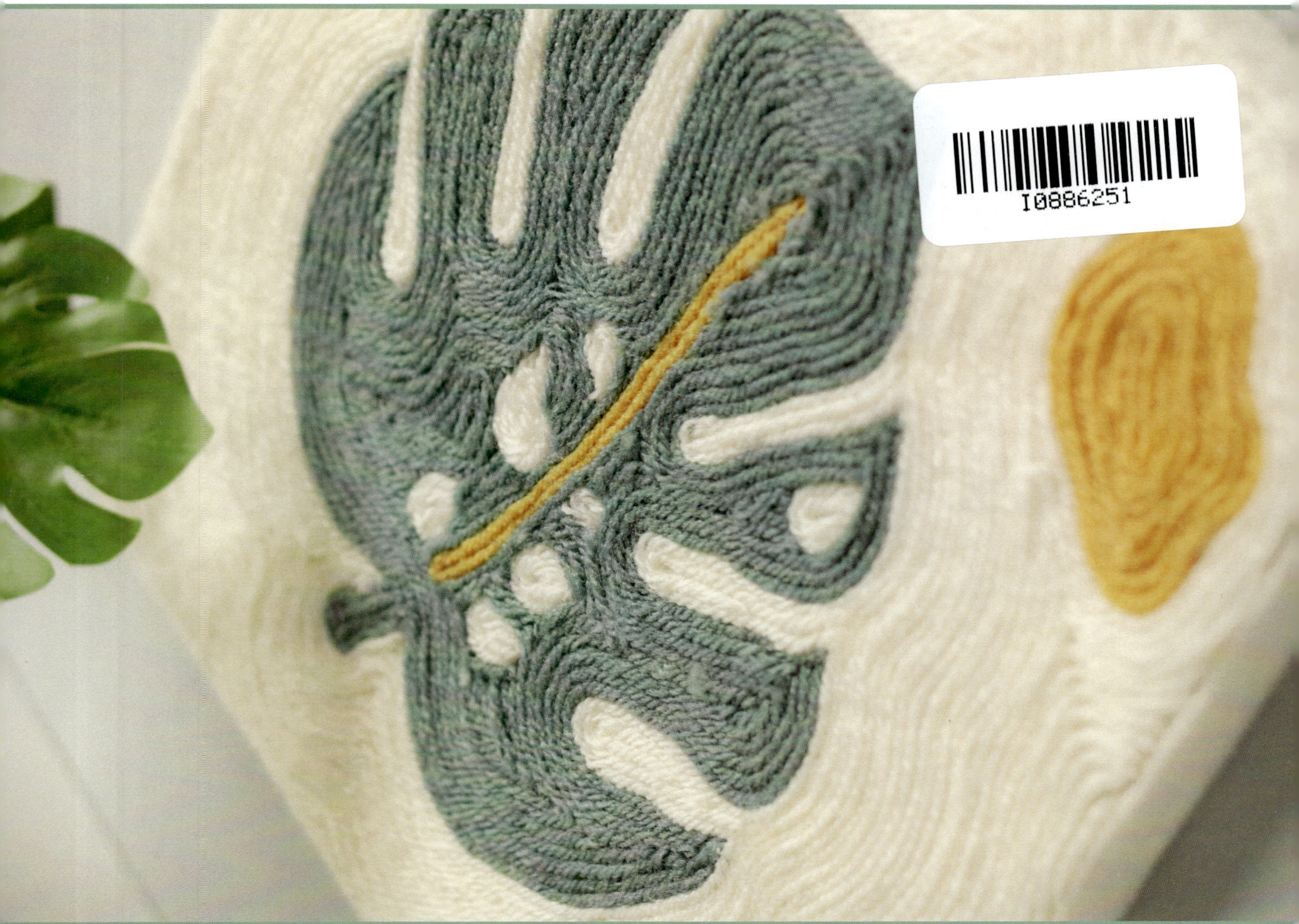

INTRODUCTION

Welcome to the world of yarn painting! It's relaxing, colorful, and provides hours of entertainment. Each project is fun to customize with color and make your own. Have fun "painting" your own rocket, hot air balloon, monstera leaf...and more! This book is suitable for adults and children and the fun can go on for hours simply painting with yarn!

Everyone can take part and create their own yarn painting! With minimal supplies, you can enjoy hours of creative fun! Bring the color of painting with yarn into your home today!

LEISURE ARTS, INC. • Maumelle, Arkansas

MEET THE AUTHOR

Inspired by her love of yarn, Kristi Simpson creates crochet, knit, macramé and weaving projects with a fresh and modern touch. The mother of five became hooked on crochet after teaching herself, so she could teach her daughter to make a scarf from a "learn to crochet" kit that was a gift.

"I loved it from the beginning!" She says, "I'm amazed that I could take a strand of yarn and create something so useful and pretty! Needless to say, I never stopped!"

She uses her love of yarn to create a range of crafts from crochet, to knitting, to weaving, and yarn painting. She also loves other crafts such as card making and scrapbooking.

Look for other Leisure Arts books featuring Kristi's designs at **www.leisurearts.com.**

TABLE OF CONTENTS

MONSTERA LEAF

SHOPPING LIST

- ☐ 12" x 12" primed canvas
- ☐ Enlarged photocopy of pattern (page 24)
- ☐ Small, sharp scissors
- ☐ Carbon transfer paper
- ☐ Pencil
- ☐ Clear-drying craft glue
- ☐ A mug to place your glue bottle in
- ☐ Paper towels
- ☐ Plastic yarn guide for laying yarn
- ☐ Lion Brand® Vanna's Choice® Yarn - 1 skein each: Sage, Fisherman, Mustard

Instructions

*Refer to **Basic Instructions**, page 30, before beginning your project.*

1. Use the carbon transfer paper and pencil to transfer the Monstera Leaf to your canvas.

2. Outline Section 1 with Sage. Fill Sections 2 with Fisherman. Fill Sections 3 with Mustard **(Fig. 1)**.

3. Working in a clockwise motion, continue to outline the inside of Section 1 **(Fig. 2)**. When filling Section 1, if the yarns begin to touch each other and leave open areas, fill each area individually **(Fig. 3)**.

4. As the yarn fills Section 1, work around each Section 2, cutting yarn as needed **(Fig. 4)**.

5. When Section 1 is completely filled, working clockwise, outline the leaf with Fisherman. As the leaf is outlined, it will create openings that need to be filled. Only fill to edge of leaf **(Fig. 5)**.

6. When the spaces around the leaf are completely filled, it is time to outline the leaf. Use Fisherman and work clockwise to outline the leaf **(Fig. 6)**. Use the yarn guide to pull in the sections to keep the grooves and shape of leaf **(Fig. 7)**.

7. Continue to outline the leaf until you reach the edge of the canvas. When the edge is reached, cut the yarn and work around the leaf **(Fig. 8)**.

8. As the outline continues, it will reach each Section 3. Work evenly around each Section 3 until canvas front is full **(Fig. 9)**.

9. Place the canvas face down. To finish sides of the canvas, add glue to sides and line each edge with rows of Fisherman, cutting yarn at one corner.

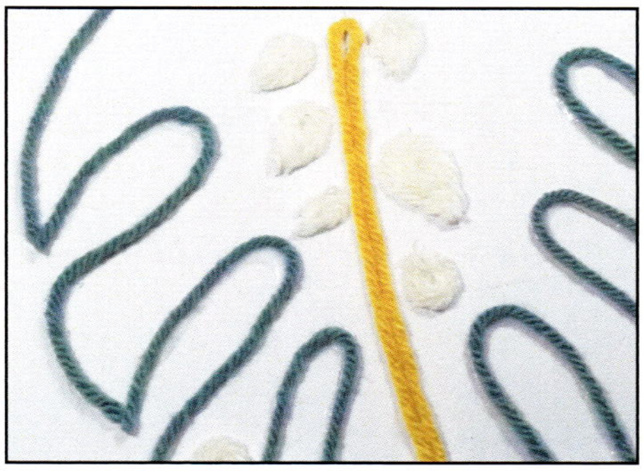

Fig. 1

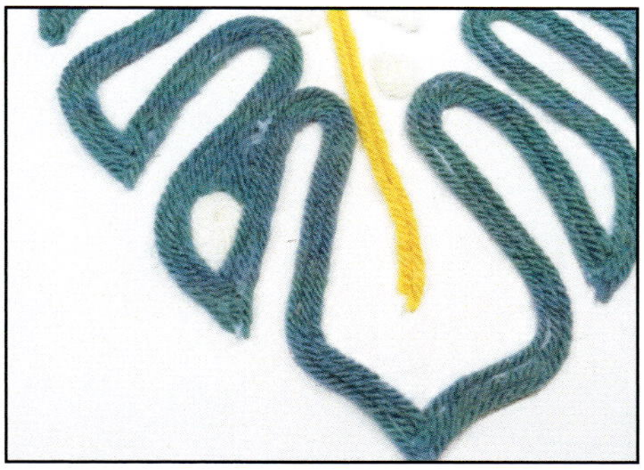

Fig. 2

Fig. 3

Fig. 4

Fig. 5

Fig. 6

Fig. 7

Fig. 8

Fig. 9

BUTTERFLY WING

SHOPPING LIST

- ☐ 12" x 12" primed canvas
- ☐ Enlarged photocopy of pattern (page 26)
- ☐ Small, sharp scissors
- ☐ Carbon transfer paper
- ☐ Pencil
- ☐ Clear-drying craft glue
- ☐ A mug to place your glue bottle in
- ☐ Paper towels
- ☐ Plastic yarn guide for laying yarn
- ☐ Lion Brand® Vanna's Choice® Yarn - 1 skein each: Rust, Black, White

Instructions

*Refer to **Basic Instructions**, page 30, before beginning your project.*

1. Use the carbon transfer paper and pencil to transfer the Butterfly Wing to your canvas.

2. Fill each Section 1 with Rust **(Fig. 1)**.

3. Cut White yarn into fifty 6" lengths. Holding many lengths together at a time, cut lengths into short lengths (less than ¼") to create "fuzz."

4. Add glue to each Section 2 and gently tap white fuzz into glue **(Fig. 2)**. This will keep it fluffy when it dries. If the fuzz settles and is too flat, repeat this step. Allow to completely dry before moving on to next steps because if it is wet, the fuzz will stick to the wet glue and black yarn and be visible.

5. Next, fill gaps between all Sections 1 with lengths of Black **(Fig. 3)**. Do not work around Sections 2 spots yet **(Fig. 4)**. Allow to dry.

6. Glue Black around Section 2 spots. Work close to the edges so that the fuzz appears 3D. If fuzz does get on the wet glue on top of black, gently remove before it dries.

7. To complete the outer edge of the canvas, add glue to front edge of canvas and lay a length of Black yarn along the edge, cutting ends at one corner. Allow to dry.

8. Place the canvas face down. To finish sides of the canvas, add glue to sides and line each edge with rows of Black, cutting yarn at one corner.

Fig. 1

Fig. 2

Fig. 3

Fig. 4

Fig. 5

ROCKET

SHOPPING LIST

- ☐ 5" x 7" primed canvas
- ☐ Enlarged photocopy of pattern (page 27)
- ☐ Small, sharp scissors
- ☐ Carbon transfer paper
- ☐ Pencil
- ☐ Clear-drying craft glue
- ☐ A mug to place your glue bottle in
- ☐ Paper towels
- ☐ Plastic yarn guide for laying yarn
- ☐ Paint - Navy
- ☐ Paintbrush
- ☐ Lion Brand® Vanna's Choice® Yarn - 1 skein each: Sky Blue, Scarlet, White, Pale Grey, Lemon, Rust

Instructions

*Refer to **Basic Instructions**, page 30, before beginning your project.*

1. Begin by painting canvas navy. Allow to dry.
2. Use the carbon transfer paper and pencil to transfer the Rocket to your canvas.
3. Begin by outlining and filling Section 1 with Sky Blue.
4. Outline Section 1 with Pale Grey.
5. Outline and fill Section 2 with White, working around Section 1.
6. Outline and fill Section 3 with Scarlet.
7. Outline the outer line of Sections 4 and 5 with Scarlet and fill each section, working inward from top to bottom.
8. Add a short length of Scarlet under Section 2.
9. Fill Section 6 with 3 short lengths of Lemon.
10. Outline Section 6 twice with short lengths of Rust.
11. Outline and fill Section 7 with Sky Blue.
12. Cut Pale Grey yarn into ten 6" lengths. Cut White yarn into ten 6" lengths. Holding all lengths together at one time, cut lengths into short lengths (less than ¼") to create "fuzz."
13. Fill Section 8 with glue and gently tap white fuzz into glue. Do not push into glue. This will keep it fluffy when it dries. If the fuzz settles and is too flat, repeat this step.

LANDSCAPE

SHOPPING LIST

- ☐ 5" x 7" primed canvas
- ☐ Enlarged photocopy of pattern (page 27)
- ☐ Small, sharp scissors
- ☐ Pencil
- ☐ Carbon transfer paper
- ☐ Pencil
- ☐ Clear-drying craft glue
- ☐ A mug to place your glue bottle in
- ☐ Paper towels
- ☐ Plastic yarn guide for laying yarn
- ☐ Lion Brand® Vanna's Choice® Yarn - 1 skein each: Olive, Charcoal Grey, Rust, Pale Grey, Mustard, Sky Blue

Instructions

*Refer to **Basic Instructions**, page 30, before beginning your project.*

1. Use the carbon transfer paper and pencil to transfer the Landscape to your canvas.

2. Outline and fill Section 1 with Olive. Start at the bottom and work to the top of the section.

3. Outline and fill Section 2 with Charcoal Grey.

4. Outline and fill Section 3 with Rust (**Fig. 1**).

5. Outline and fill Section 4 with Pale Grey.

6. Outline and fill Section 5 with Charcoal Grey.

7. Outline and fill Section 6 with Olive.

8. Outline and fill Section 7 with Rust.

9. Outline and fill Section 8 with Pale Grey.

10. Outline and fill Section 9 with Charcoal Grey.

11. Outline and fill Section 10 with Olive.

12. Outline and fill Section 11 with Rust (**Fig. 2**).

13. Outline and fill Section 12 with Mustard in a clockwise direction.

14. Outline and fill Sections 13 and 14 with Sky Blue. Outline Section 12 and start at the bottom and work to the top of each section.

15. Add glue to front edge of canvas and lay lengths of corresponding color yarn along the edge to create a frame. Allow to dry.

Fig. 1

Fig. 2

ABSTRACT WAVES

SHOPPING LIST

- ☐ 8" x 10" primed canvas
- ☐ Enlarged photocopy of pattern (page 29)
- ☐ Small, sharp scissors
- ☐ Carbon transfer paper
- ☐ Pencil
- ☐ Clear-drying craft glue
- ☐ A mug to place your glue bottle in
- ☐ Paper towels
- ☐ Plastic yarn guide for laying yarn
- ☐ Premier® Anti-Pilling Everyday® Worsted Yarn - 1 skein each: Spa, Glass, Cream, Peacock, Soft Peach

Instructions

*Refer to **Basic Instructions**, page 30, before beginning your project. To fill sections, work in numerical order.*

1. Use the carbon transfer paper and pencil to transfer the Abstract Waves to your canvas.
2. Outline and fill Section 1 with Cream.
3. Outline and fill Section 2 with Soft Peach.
4. Outline and fill Section 3 with Peacock.
5. Outline and fill Section 4 with Spa.
6. Outline and fill Section 5 with Glass.
7. Outline and fill Section 6 with Spa.
8. Outline and fill Section 7 with Cream.
9. Outline and fill Section 8 with Peacock.
10. Outline and fill Section 9 with Soft Peach.
11. Outline and fill Section 10 with Spa.
12. Outline and fill Section 11 with Cream.
13. Outline and fill Section 12 with Glass.
14. Outline and fill Section 13 with Soft Peach.
15. Outline and fill Section 14 with Cream.
16. Outline and fill Section 15 with Spa.
17. Outline and fill Section 16 with Peacock.
18. Outline and fill Section 17 with Glass.
19. Outline and fill Section 18 with Spa.
20. Add glue to front edge of canvas and lay lengths of corresponding color yarn along the edge to create a frame. Allow to dry.

LAVENDER BASKET

SHOPPING LIST

- ☐ 8" x 10" primed canvas
- ☐ Enlarged photocopy of pattern (page 28)
- ☐ Small, sharp scissors
- ☐ Carbon transfer paper
- ☐ Pencil
- ☐ Clear-drying craft glue
- ☐ A mug to place your glue bottle in
- ☐ Paper towels
- ☐ Plastic yarn guide for laying yarn
- ☐ Lion Brand® Basic Stitch Anti Pill Yarn - 1 skein each: Purple, Prism, Charcoal Heather, Gold Heather
- ☐ Lion Brand® Vanna's Choice® Yarn - 1 skein each: Chocolate, Fern

Instructions

Refer to ***Basic Instructions****, page 30, before beginning your project.*

1. Use the carbon transfer paper and pencil to transfer the Lavender Basket to your canvas.

2. Outline Section 1 and the lines inside Section 1 in Chocolate **(Fig. 1)**.

3. Fill the inside of the box with Gold Heather **(Fig. 2)**.

4. Fill Section 2 with Fern. Work with 2 strips of yarn at a time, pointing them in the same direction. Add the pairs at different heights across the top of the box **(Fig. 3)**.

5. Cut Purple and Prism yarns into 6" lengths **(Fig. 4)**. Holding groups of lengths together at one time, cut lengths into short lengths (less than ¼") **(Fig. 5)** to create "fuzz."

6. Fill Section 3 with glue and gently tap fuzz into glue **(Fig. 6)**. Do not push into glue. This will keep it fluffy when it dries. If the fuzz settles and is too flat, repeat this step. Continue adding the purple mix in sections across the top of Section 2 **(Fig. 7)**. Allow to dry.

7. For decorative border, align Charcoal Heather lengths on each side of basket. Cut 2" past edge of canvas **(Fig. 8)**. Allow to dry. This will be wrapped to the back of the canvas after the front dries.

8. Flip canvas with front down. Glue the yarn ends to back of the canvas and trim **(Fig. 9)**.

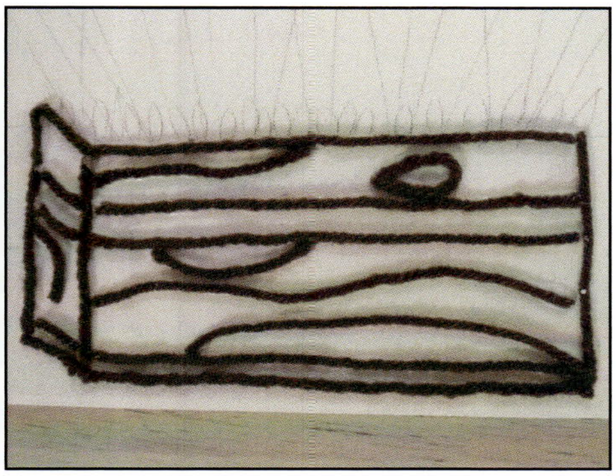
Fig. 1

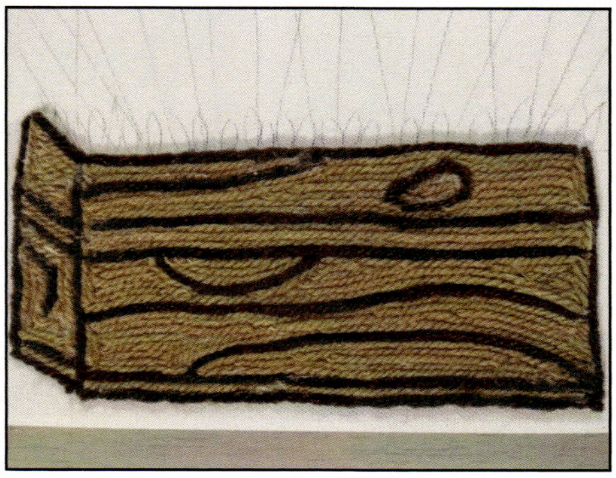
Fig. 2

Fig. 3

Fig. 4

Fig. 5

Fig. 6

Fig. 7

Fig. 8

Fig.9

CACTUS

SHOPPING LIST

- ☐ 8" x 10" primed canvas
- ☐ Enlarged photocopy of pattern (page 29)
- ☐ Small, sharp scissors
- ☐ Carbon transfer paper
- ☐ Pencil
- ☐ Clear-drying craft glue
- ☐ A mug to place your glue bottle in
- ☐ Paper towels
- ☐ Plastic yarn guide for laying yarn
- ☐ Lion Brand® Heartland Yarn - 1 skein each: Saguaro (Green), Yosemite (Rust), Great Sand Dunes (Tan), Mount Rainier (Gray), Cuyahoga Valley (Teal), Isle Royale (Purple), Yellowstone (yellow), Biscayne (Pink)

Instructions

*Refer to **Basic Instructions**, page 30, before beginning your project.*

1. Use the carbon transfer paper and pencil to transfer the Cactus to your canvas.
2. Outline and fill Section 1 in Saguaro (**Fig. 1**).
3. Outline and fill Section 2 in Yosemite from the bottom to top to create a "hill" effect (**Fig. 2**).
4. Fill Sections 3 and 4 with Great Sand Dunes (**Fig. 3**).
5. Fill Sections 5 and 6 with Mount Rainier from bottom to top.
6. Fill Sections 7 and 8 with Cuyahoga Valley from bottom to top.
7. Skip Section 9 at this time.
8. Fill Section 10-12 with Isle Royale.
9. Skip Section 13 at this time.
10. Fill Section 14 with Biscayne.
11. Skip Section 15 at this time.
12. Fill Section 16 with Yellowstone.
13. Fill Section 17 with Yosemite.
14. Allow to dry.
15. To fill Section 9, alternate colors to complete Chevron pattern, placing 4 strands at a time with Biscayne and Yellowstone. Use the yarn guide to help create the direction of the chevron.
16. Fill each teardrop in Section 13 with Cuyahoga Valley; allow to dry. Fill the remaining Section around the teardrops with Great Sand Dunes.
17. Outline Section 16 two times with Isle Royale.
18. Outline the petals in Section 15 two times with Isle Royale. Fill the inside of the petals with Mount Rainier. Fill the outside of the flower petals with Yosemite.
19. Add glue to front edge of canvas and lay lengths of corresponding color yarn along the edge to create a frame. Allow to dry.
20. Place the canvas face down. To finish sides of the canvas, add glue to sides and line each edge with rows of Yosemite, cutting yarn at one corner.

Fig. 1

Fig. 2

Fig. 3

HOT AIR BALLOON

SHOPPING LIST

- ☐ 8" x 10" primed canvas
- ☐ Enlarged photocopy of pattern (page 29)
- ☐ Small, sharp scissors
- ☐ Carbon transfer paper
- ☐ Pencil
- ☐ Clear-drying craft glue
- ☐ A mug to place your glue bottle in
- ☐ Paper towels
- ☐ Plastic yarn guide for laying yarn
- ☐ Lion Brand Vanna's Choice Yarn - 1 skein each: Fern, Olive, Chocolate, White, Electric Blue, Sky Blue, Lemon, Pale Grey, Scarlet Red

Fig. 1

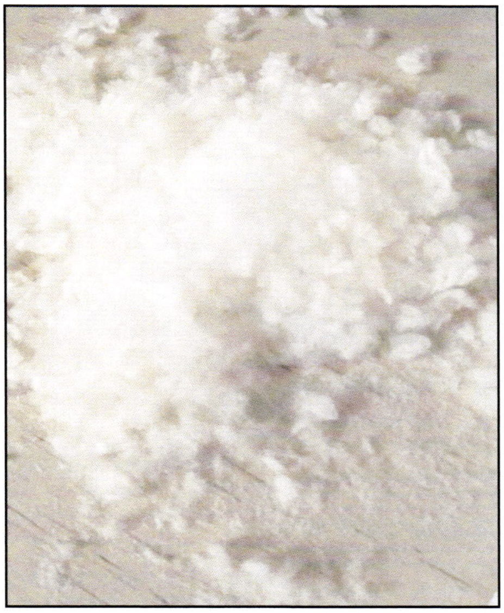

Fig. 2

Fig. 3

Fig. 4

Fig. 5

Instructions

*Refer to **Basic Instructions**, page 30, before beginning your project.*

1. Use the carbon transfer paper and pencil to transfer the Hot Air Balloon to your canvas.

2. Cut White yarn into twenty 6" lengths **(Fig. 1)**. Holding all lengths together at a time, cut lengths into short lengths (less than ¼") **(Fig. 2)** to create "fuzz."

3. Add glue to each Section 1 and gently tap white fuzz into glue **(Fig. 3)**. This will keep it fluffy when it dries. If the fuzz settles and is too flat, repeat this step. Allow to dry.

4. Outline **(Fig. 4)** and fill Section 2 with Fern.

5. Outline and fill each Sections 3 with Olive **(Fig. 5)**

Instructions (Continued)

6. Outline Section 4, including the "ropes" that stretch up to the ballon with Chocolate. Work from top to bottom to fill the Section **(Fig. 6)**.

7. Outline and fill Sections 5, including the section above the basket, with Sky Blue **(Fig. 7)**.

8. Outline and fill Sections 6 and 7 with Electric Blue.

9. Outline and fill Section 8 with Sky Blue **(Fig. 8)**.

10. Outline and fill Sections 9 and 10 with Lemon in a zig-zag design. Fill the section at the bottom of the balloon with Lemon **(Fig. 9)**.

11. Fill Sections 11-19 with Scarlet Red **(Fig. 10)**.

12. Fill Sections 20-31 with Pale Grey.

13. After balloon is complete, add a line of glue around each cloud **(Fig. 11)** and add a little bit of white fuzz mix to extend the cloud to blend into the background.

Fig. 6

Fig. 7

Fig. 8

Fig. 9

Fig. 10

Fig. 11

GUITAR

SHOPPING LIST

- ☐ 12" x 12" primed canvas
- ☐ Enlarged photocopy of pattern (page 25)
- ☐ Small, sharp scissors
- ☐ Carbon transfer paper
- ☐ Pencil
- ☐ Clear-drying craft glue
- ☐ A mug to place your glue bottle in
- ☐ Paper towels
- ☐ Plastic yarn guide for laying yarn
- ☐ Premier® Ever Soft® Yarn - 1 skein each: Cocoa, Taupe, Cream, Denim, Yellow, Icy Blue, Mist

Instructions

*Refer to **Basic Instructions**, page 30, before beginning your project.*

1. Use the carbon transfer paper and pencil to transfer the Guitar to your canvas.

2. Fill Section 1 vertically with Cocoa. **(Fig. 1)**

3. Working clockwise, fill Section 2 with Cocoa. Leave a space between Sections 1 and 2 **(Fig. 2)**. Fill Section 3 with about 5 horizontal lengths of Cocoa. Outline Section 3 with one round of Cocoa. Using Taupe, add a vertical line on left edge of Section 1. Outline Sections 2 and 3 using Taupe **(Fig. 3)**.

4. Starting on right edge, fill Section 4 with long vertical lengths of Cream. Fill until you reach the right side of Section 3. Keep yarn lengths close together **(Fig. 4)**. Continue filling below Section 3 with vertical lengths of Cream until the left edge of Section 3 is reached **(Fig. 5)**. Continue filling Section 4 until complete. Outline Section 4 with 1 Round of Taupe and 2 Rounds of Cocoa **(Fig. 6)**. Allow to dry.

Fig. 1

Fig. 2

Fig. 3

Fig. 4

Fig. 5

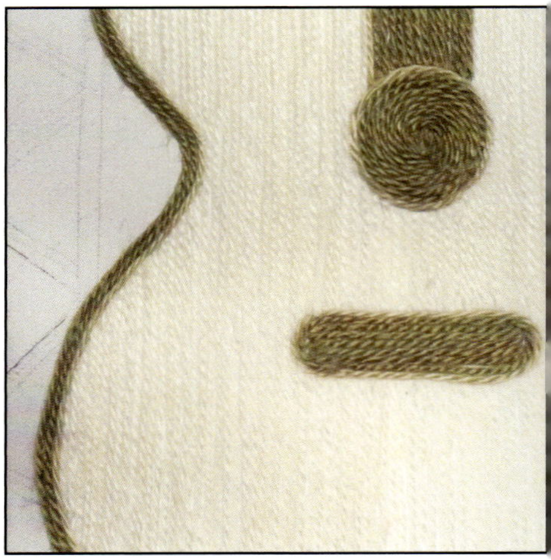

Fig. 6

Instructions (Continued)

5. Beginning at bottom, fill Section 5 in the following order: Icy Blue, Yellow, Denim. I used 10 lengths of yarn for each side of each chevron. Make sure the yarn lengths are evenly cut in the center and at the sides **(Fig. 7)**.

6. Fill Sections 6, 7 and 8 with lengths of Denim **(Fig. 8)**.

7. Fill Section 9 according to pattern. Start with the yellow triangles on left. Then add one line each of Denim, Icy Blue and then Denim. Fill remaining triangles on right with Yellow.

8. Fill the Sections 10, 11, and 12 with horizontal lengths of Icy Blue.

9. Now, the Guitar should be dry. Add 8 short horizontal lengths on Section 1 in Mist. Allow to dry.

10. Add 6 vertical lengths of Mist from the top of canvas to Section 3 for the guitar strings; trim evenly **(Fig. 9)**.

11. Add a short length of Taupe along ends of strings **(Fig. 10)**.

12. Add glue to front edge of canvas and lay lengths of corresponding color yarn along the edge to create a frame. Allow to dry.

Fig. 7

Fig. 8

Fig. 9

Fig. 10

PATTERNS

MONSTERA LEAF - From Page 4 - Enlarge this image 160%

GUITAR - From Page 21 - Enlarge this image 160%

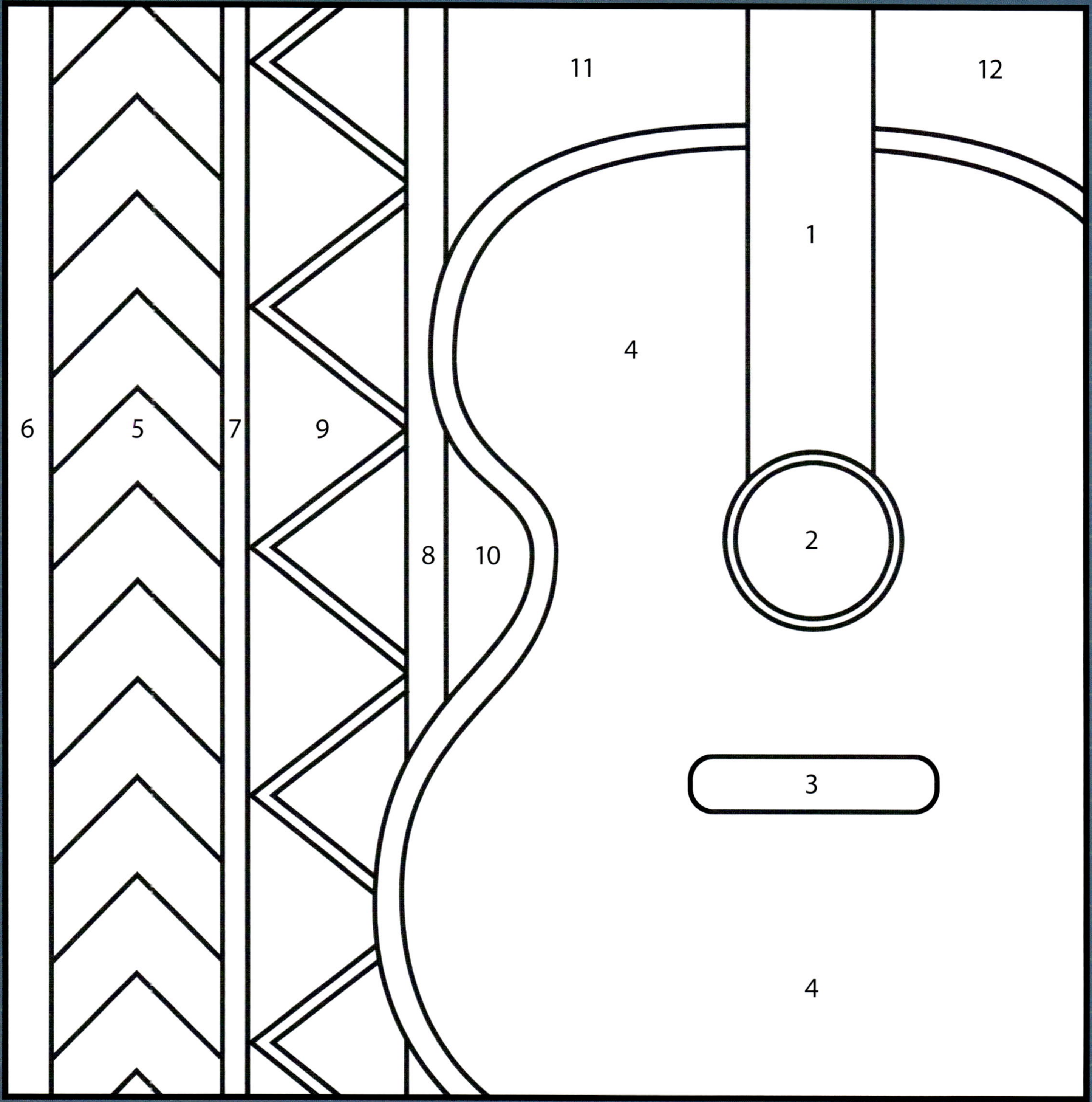

BUTTERFLY WING - From Page 6

Enlarge this image 160%

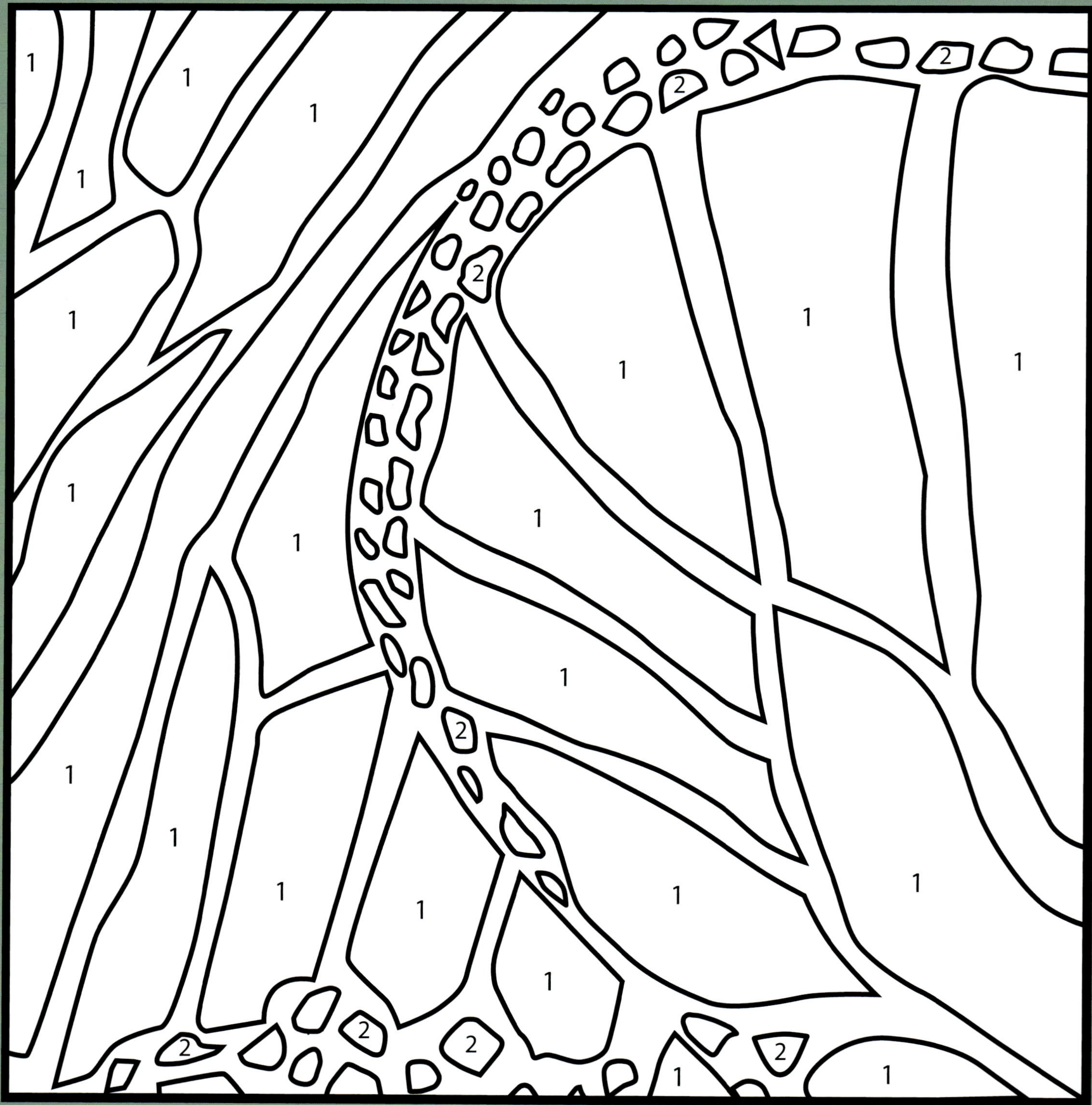

ROCKET - From Page 8
Enlarge this image 133%

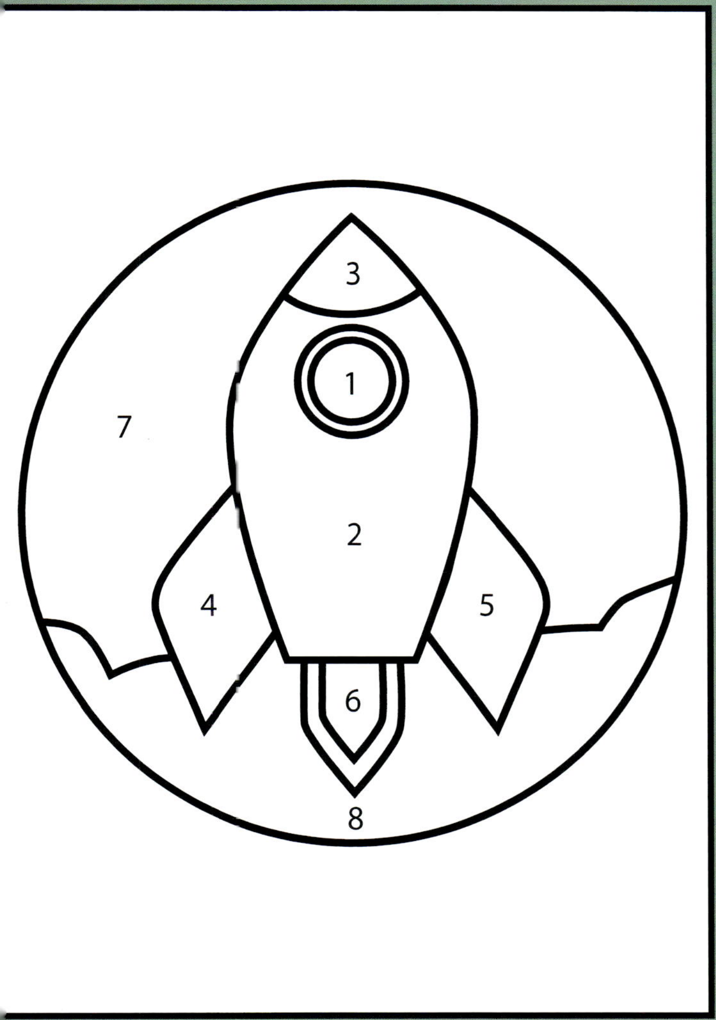

LANDSCAPE - From Page 10
Enlarge this image 133%

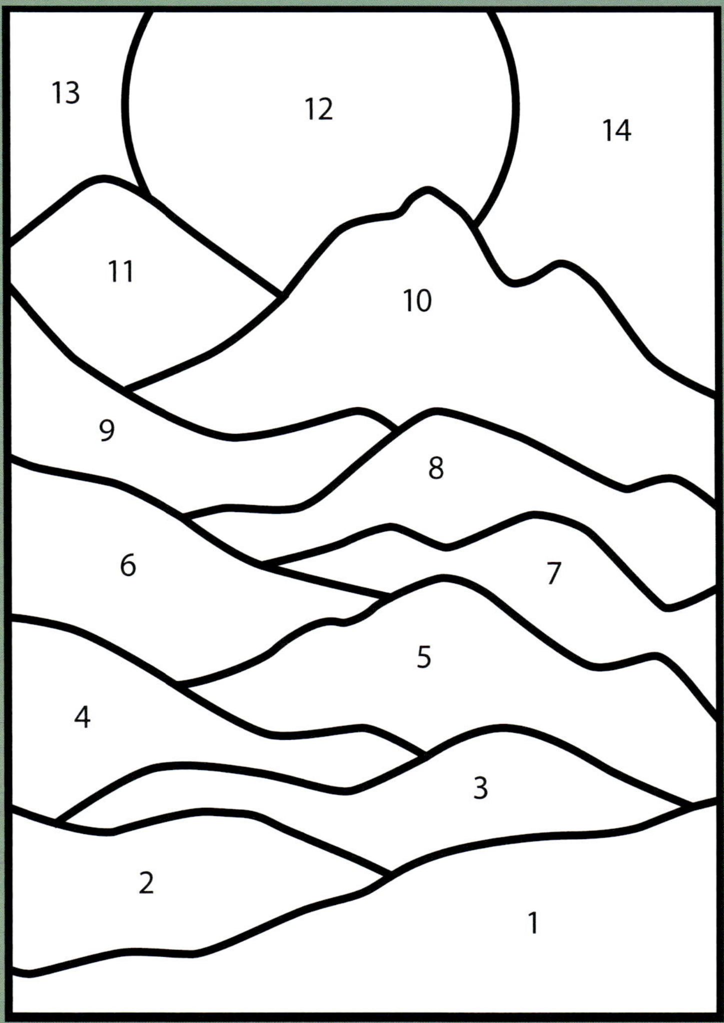

LAVENDER BASKET - From Page 14 - Enlarge this image 113%

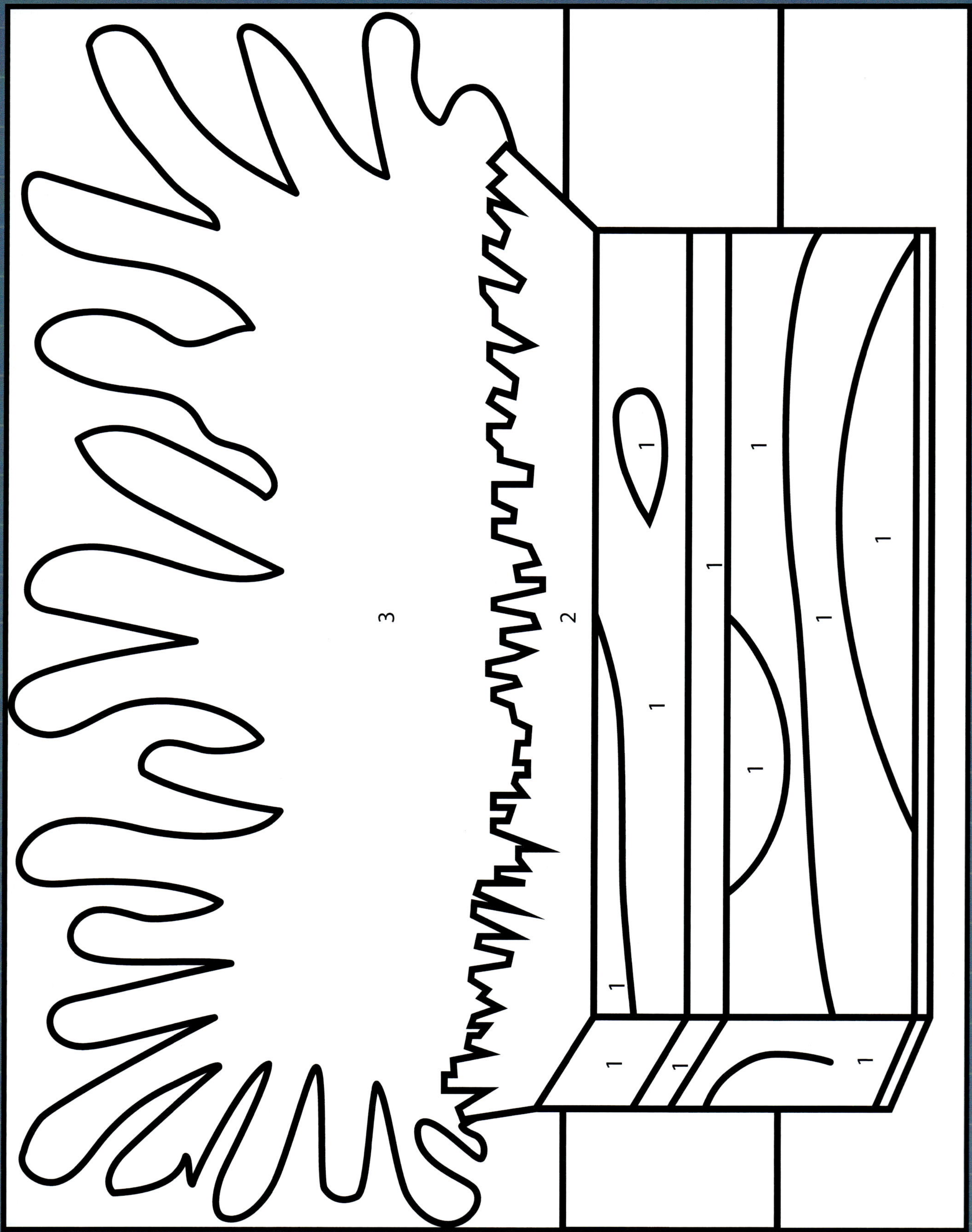

ABSTRACT WAVES - From Page 12
Enlarge this image 250%

CACTUS - From Page 16
Enlarge this image 250%

HOT AIR BALOON - From Page 18
Enlarge this image 250%

Fig. 1

Fig. 2

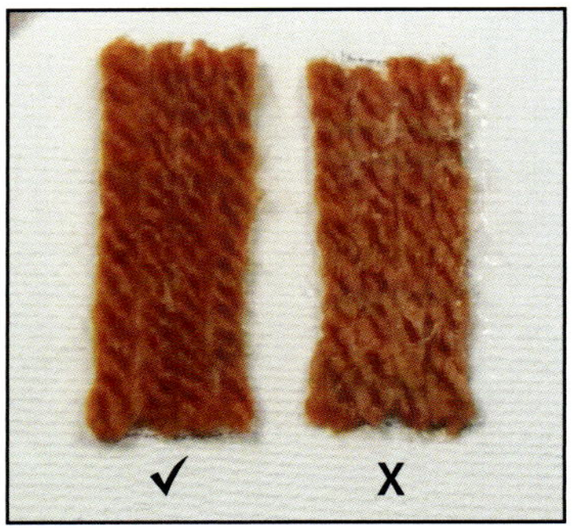

Fig. 3

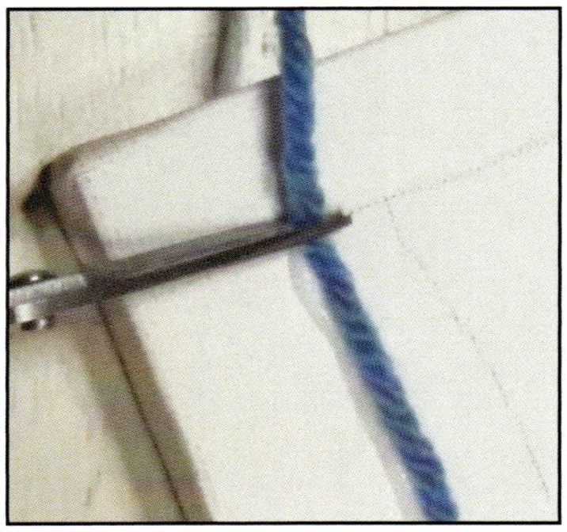
Fig. 4

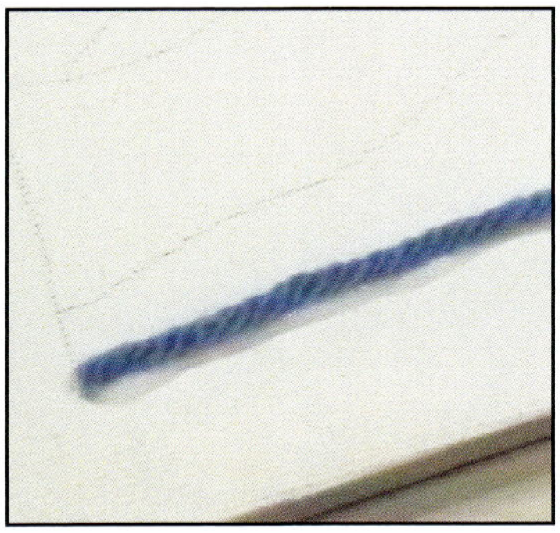
Fig. 5

Basic Instructions

1. Center pattern over canvas with carbon transfer paper sandwiched in between. Trace over lines on pattern to transfer outlines to canvas.

2. To outline the section, lay down a straight line of glue to cover the transferred base line **(Fig. 1)**.

TIP: Use a lot of glue. This works in your favor! You can move the yarn now and later as it's drying. The yarn will soak it up, so feel free to add more as needed.

3. Use the yarn guide to help lay the yarn over the glue **(Fig. 2)**.

TIP: When you're placing the yarn, lightly tap the yarn in place. Do not push the yarn flat into the glue. If you do, then the yarn will soak up the glue, and it will not stay fluffy on top as you see in the photos. It will be flat and hard and even a different color (darker usually) because it will appear *wet*. So, gently tap-tap-tap-tap... not SQUISH (Fig. 3)!

4. Cut yarn even with transferred line **(Fig. 4)**. The yarn end should align with the line **(Fig. 5)**.

5. Lay down a line of glue above the yarn **(Fig. 6)**. Lay yarn close to the previous line **(Fig. 7)**. You may see glue between the yarn but you do not want large gaps.

6. To fill the sections, continue to layer glue and yarn, cutting along the edge of the transferred lines on the canvas **(Fig. 8)**

7. To complete the section, start on one edge and lay down a line of glue **(Fig. 9)**. To outline the section, add yarn and use yarn guide to push yarn close to cut yarn ends. As the glue dries, you can manipulate the yarn to be even closer **(Fig.10)**.

8. Now that the first section is complete, let's move on to the next section. To outline the section, lay a line of

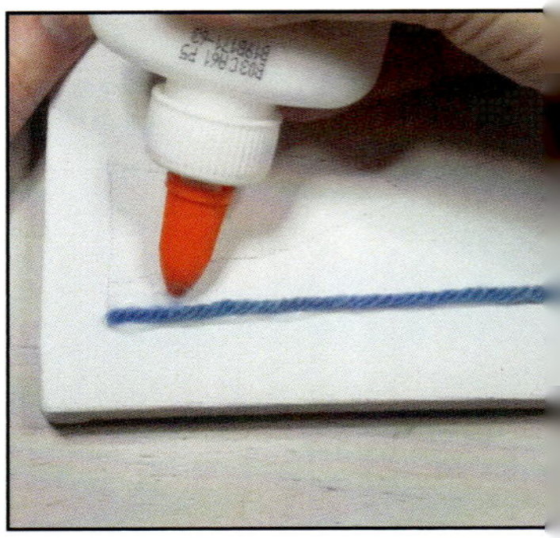
Fig. 6

Fig. 7

Fig. 8

Fig. 9

Fig. 10

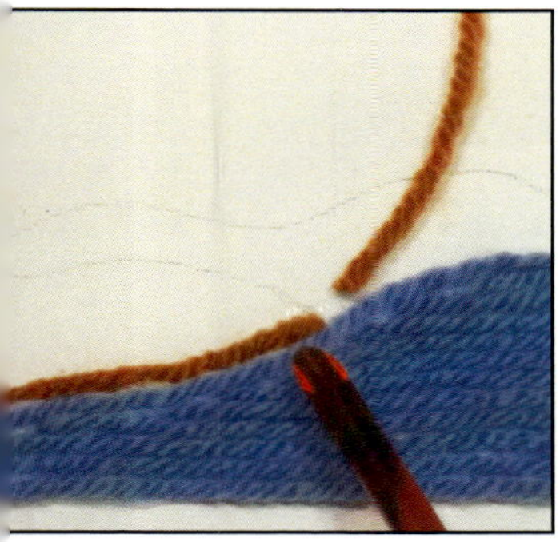
Fig. 11

Fig. 12

Fig. 13

Fig. 14

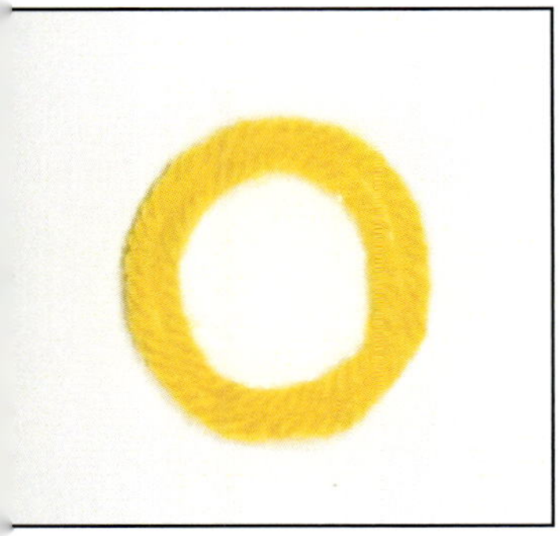
Fig. 15

glue along the edge. To fill the section, use the next color, starting the yarn on the outside edge and trimming the yarn on the inside transferred line (**Fig. 11**). Continue to layer glue and yarn until section is filled (**Fig. 12**).

TIP: One of the biggest tips, I could offer, is to start your yarn on the outside and trim on the inside when possible. This will make your edges straighter. If you have to cut each end of yarn on the outside edge, it is difficult to get the edge to be clean and straight. Once the glue is down, it is easier to pull the edges even.

9. Repeat Step 7 to complete the area (**Fig. 13**).

10. To outline a circle, lay down the glue along the transferred line. Place the yarn over the glue and cut end as close as possible to beginning end. Use yarn guide to move yarn over line (**Fig. 14**). Fill the circle on the inside, trimming ends evenly and using yarn guide to push yarn lines together closely (**Fig. 15**). To fill the center, lay down glue, lay yarn down, and cut a small piece (**Fig. 16**).

11. When working with angles, like the areas on each side of the hot air balloon basket, rocket fins or the inside of the butterfly wings, you'll need to make sharp, clean cuts to create the correct shape. Let's take a look at creating a triangle to break down the angles. Remember, the yarn can be moved and stretched and you can fray the ends a bit to fill in corners. To outline the section, start by adding glue over the transferred line and laying the first line of yarn (**Fig. 17**). Cut along the transferred line at an angle. Continue around the shape (**Fig. 18**). The angle may not always be a triangle, but could involve sharp angles that need more attention than just a curved yarn.

12. Fill the inside of the angle, cutting yarn at an angle at each corner (**Fig. 19**). Continue until the space is filled (**Fig. 20**). To fill the center, lay down glue, lay yarn down, and cut a small piece.

Fig. 16

Fig. 17

Fig. 18

Fig. 19

Fig. 20

TIPS FOR YARN PAINTING

• Do not use a tightly woven yarn like mercerized cotton. You want the yarn to be loosely twisted with little bits of fibers to stick to the glue and blend into small sections. Tightly twisted yarns will be more difficult to blend together.

• Throughout the instructions, you will not be instructed to add glue each time it's necessary. Instead the instructions will read, for example, "Outline Section 1 in Blue." It is understood that you will add glue and then outline with the blue yarn.

• Use clear-drying craft glue. Each project uses 2-4 oz of glue; depending on size of canvas and painting.

• Place your glue bottle upside down in a mug and it will be ready for use each time you need it - no shaking that bottle!

• As the glue is drying, the yarn is still moveable. Adjust yarn lines as needed to hide spaces. I use a plastic "yarn guide" for laying yarn. I use the end of an angled paintbrush. A plastic manicure utensil is also a good guide. Do not use wood. The glue and yarn fibers will stick to the wood and it is not as easy to clean as a plastic tip.

• Use a small pair of sharp scissors Embroidery scissors are recommended.

• If you want, paint the background areas of the canvas using acrylic paint in colors similar to the yarn colors being used. If there are gaps between your yarn strands, the white canvas will not show through. I did not do this in my projects, and it looks fine without, too!

Each project lists the specific yarns used to create our photography models. Because yarn manufacturers make frequent changes in their product lines, you may sometimes find it necessary to use a substitute yarn or to search for the discontinued product at alternate suppliers (locally or online).

Production Team: Publishing Manager - Megan Copeland; Technical Editor – Lisa Lancaster; Graphic Artist – Michael Puckett; Photographer – Rob Karman.

Made in U.S.A.